The TEN Commandments

Exodus 20:1–17

Written by Claire Miller
Illustrated by Yoshi Miyake

CONCORDIA PUBLISHING HOUSE · SAINT LOUIS

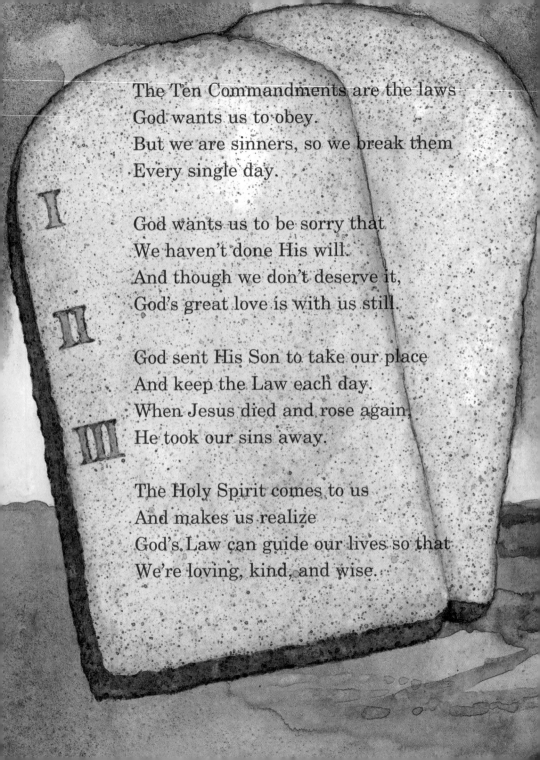

The Ten Commandments are the laws
God wants us to obey.
But we are sinners, so we break them
Every single day.

God wants us to be sorry that
We haven't done His will.
And though we don't deserve it,
God's great love is with us still.

God sent His Son to take our place
And keep the Law each day.
When Jesus died and rose again,
He took our sins away.

The Holy Spirit comes to us
And makes us realize
God's Law can guide our lives so that
We're loving, kind, and wise.

God gave His laws to Moses on
A mountain long ago.
These Ten Commandments are God's gift.
They're something we should know.

They help us live a godly life,
And show us what to do.
Now, listen to what God has to say
About them just to you.

"I am your one and only God,
And I'll take care of you.
I love you more than you can know.
Now love and trust Me too."

1 First Commandment:
You shall have no other gods.

"Do not misuse My holy name
To lie or curse or swear.
Instead call on Me any time
In praise and thanks and prayer."

2 Second Commandment:
You shall not misuse the name of
the Lord your God.

"At church, at home, at Sunday school,
You hear My holy Word,
Receive forgiveness in My gifts
And message you have heard."

3 Third Commandment:
    Remember the Sabbath day by
keeping it holy.

"Your parents and your teacher give
You loving care each day.
Respect all leaders, love them too,
And willingly obey."

4 Fourth Commandment:
    Honor your father and your mother.

"Do what you can to keep folks safe.
Protect them when you can.
And don't get even, hate, or hurt.
That isn't in My plan."

5 Fifth Commandment:
You shall not murder.

"Respect each other, girls and boys.
And don't be crude or mean.
Forget those dirty, shameful words.
Keep thoughts and actions clean."

6   Sixth Commandment:
        You shall not commit adultery.

"It's wrong to steal; instead protect
Each other's property.
Since I've created everything,
You're doing it for Me."

7 Seventh Commandment:
You shall not steal.

"When people lie, their words can hurt
Themselves and others too.
Be kind and thoughtful when you speak,
And always say what's true."

Eighth Commandment:
   You shall not give false testimony
against your neighbor.

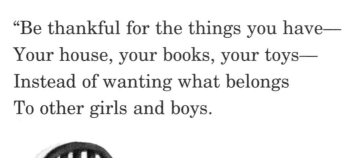

"Be thankful for the things you have—
Your house, your books, your toys—
Instead of wanting what belongs
To other girls and boys.

9 Ninth Commandment:
You shall not covet your
neighbor's house.

"Encourage people that you know
And help them get along.
Help them to keep what's rightly theirs
And keep their friendships strong."

Tenth Commandment:
    You shall not covet your neighbor's
10 wife, or his manservant or maidservant,
    his ox or donkey, or anything that belongs
    to your neighbor.

God's Law is perfect; we are not.
In sin we would be lost.
But Jesus has redeemed us all
At an amazing cost!

It is through God's great power alone
We're rescued, and set free
To live as children of the Lord,
Now and eternally!

Dear Parents,

God's Ten Commandments are a blessing and a gift. They are like a friendly fence that keeps us from falling into a deep canyon. They warn of danger and show us how to get along with others. They help keep order in the world.

Most important, the commandments show us our sin. God wants us to keep His commandments perfectly and promises punishment for those who don't. The problem is—we are far from perfect. That's why God sent His Son, Jesus, to keep the Law and to take the punishment for our sins in our place. The Holy Spirit gives us faith to believe this Gospel message.

In Matthew 22:37–39, Jesus summarized the Ten Commandments in two parts: "Love the Lord your God with all your heart and with all your soul and with all your mind. This is the first and greatest commandment. And the second is like it: Love your neighbor as yourself." The important word in these verses is "love."

Remind your children that although we can't keep the law perfectly, we can let the commandments guide us in a life of love for God and for all people. And we can remember that God provides a solution for our sin: we are forgiven and redeemed through Christ.

The Author